BEYOND THE CORDONS

SELECTED POEMS

BEYOND THE CORDONS

SELECTED POEMS

Gábor Schein

Translated from the Hungarian
by Ottilie Mulzet & Erika Mihálycsa

Contra Mundum Press   New York · London · Melbourne

This is a translation of selected poems from *Üveghal* [Glass Fish] (Magvető Kiadó, 2001); *Panaszénekek* [Songs of Complaint] (Jelenkor Kiadó, 2005); *Éjszaka, utazás* [Night, Travel] (Kalligram Kiadó, 2011); and *Üdvözlet a kontinens belsejéből* [Greetings from the Interior of the Continent] (Jelenkor Kiadó, 2017). The poems "novemberi," "a betűk alól is," "Éjszakai utazás," "A sziget süllyedése," and "Ajándék a halálnak" were originally published in *Élet és irodalom*. "Por," "Harmadnapja egyfolytában," and "Erdők éjszakája" were originally published in *Jelenkor: irodalmi és művészeti folyóirat*. All poems © 2024 Gábor Schein. English translations © 2024 Erika Mihálycsa & © 2024 Ottilie Mulzet.

First Contra Mundum Press edition 2024.

All Rights Reserved under International & Pan-American Copyright Conventions.

No part of this book may be reproduced in any form or by any electronic means, including information storage and retrieval systems, without permission in writing from the publisher, except by a reviewer who may quote brief passages in a review.

Library of Congress Cataloguing-in-Publication Data

> Schein, Gábor, 1969–
> Beyond the Cordons / Gábor Schein
>
> —1st Contra Mundum Press Edition
>
> 188 pp., 5 × 8 in.

ISBN 9781940625713

I. Schein, Gábor.
II. Title.
III. Mihálycsa, Erika, & Mulzet, Ottilie.
IV. Translators.

2024944979

Ottilie Mulzet would like to extend her profound gratitude to the Hungarian Translators' House in Balatonfüred, Hungary, where some of these poems were first translated, as well as Adéla Procházková and the estate of Emila Medková for the kind permission to use her photograph *Explosion* (1959).

CONTENTS

1	Beyond the Cordons
5	Night Journey
9	Captain Cornelius's Letter ...
13	Note on the Back of a Map
16	Preparation for the Crows' Feast
17	Eyes Turned Inside Out
21	Atropos's Scissors
24	Your Sirens
26	With Silent Flight
28	The Street's Inlet
30	Canvases of Time
32	Above the Gravel Path
34	In Lightning's Flare
38	After the Iron Age
40	Farewell, Russian Style
42	Margin
45	To My Dead
47	Pebble
51	Ghost Homeland
55	Preparations for a City
60	Plunge
64	Diagrams in the River
65	Hungary, Eternal Ellipsis
67	Dawn Light
69	The Taste of Salt
74	Invisible War
76	November
77	Gravel and Reeds

79	Offering to Death
82	From Beneath the Letters
83	Third Day Unceasingly
86	The Star of Time
87	Sinking Island
89	Dust
91	Night of Forests
93	Against Phantoms
95	It Will Shine
97	Amount of Earth
102	Summer Rain, Transparent Borders
109	In the Jewish Cemetery in Worms
111	Double Inundations
113	The Color of Pain
114	The Cardinal Directions
117	Under the Bat's Wing
119	Greetings from the Interior of the Continent
121	Trench
123	Come Back
126	Fear
127	Beyond the Open Window
129	Sheath
131	New Century
133	Near
135	Light of Night-Time
137	Return of the Letters
140	Love, Sail, Time
142	Rending
156	Previous Publications
158	Biographies

GÁBOR SCHEIN · BEYOND THE CORDONS

BEYOND THE CORDONS

There were corners, blockaded squares, where, for days after the routed demonstration,
the biting smell of teargas was palpable. If the burnt-out car wrecks
and ripped-up cobblestones had been removed, still, the missing pavement
let no one forget: the city center was a zone of uncertainty.
Evening belonged to the sirens, arsonists' chants —
the squares were traps, the streets borders, trajectories of escape shut down
in a commander's head: after so many years of peace, finally able to wage war.

*

No matter where one turned, there were bars, cordons. The buildings'
stoic grey arrived from farther away than moonlight; the city spoke
of new wrath in the dead language of ornamental statuary: Poseidon is the chief god here,
in the continent's centre, where in narrow rented rooms people bargain

for stolen love. The naked stone bodies turned towards each other, like computer screens left on by mistake: the thick poppyseed of visual static sprinkled onto them, as down below, far from every sea, wrath gathered up legions of children.

*

You write the story of your body with two hands that do not know each other, two voices summon the unknown within you. Gather up the distinctions. Place the blossoming bouquet of lies, explanations, and objections onto your grave, tend your grave, clear away the beliefs falling onto it like autumn foliage. Do not look at the everyday with everyday eyes. The simplest questions are the ones you don't ask, and if someone screams into your ear, ignore them till you have run out of time.

*

In peacetime, the city centre covers its self-hatred with decorative flagstones, flower-boxes, ordered transportation; decommissioned streetcars, carrying the scent of humans from the ever more terrifying outer districts, are led to its terminal caverns. Life here was never anything else than the art of the too-slow massacre. Going along the cordons, now at last the alert mind can play with dreams of public hangings, schizophrenic love and suchlike, and believe, intoxicated, that it is engaging in politics.

*

Sometimes it is necessary to wage war. After all, deep within, relations were never peaceful. A single person is too narrow a space for so many wants and desires.
He who has no eyes and ears, always cheerful in others' presence, with owlish eyes, walking with a millstone around his neck, who, for simplicity's sake, calls himself "I."
None of them inhabit this world. All betray themselves.
Their state is emergency, and yet they may delight in their own defeat.
The one speaking here decrees against them in vain.

*

What is my problem? Someone who shares my birthday, who's known me at least twenty years, asked: Closing time? Hopelessness? Boredom?

And looked at me, as if explanations meant something. In exchange, I told a story about a grey heron I once saw in a seaside city; it stood every morning on the roof of a red Peugeot in the parking lot, waiting for fish to be thrown from the upper floor of the house opposite. Every morning, this selfsame, unlikely presence exposed to the day. Take this heron as a comparison, I said. For whatever you want.

*

If one day you leave, throw no coins over your shoulder. Grow the ice within yourself, as if sitting, eyes closed, on the other side of the moon; practice the art of slow murder. You were never anything else but the astronaut of your feelings. Your spaceship is a piece of blank paper. Do not pity those below displaying their scars after battle, and who, never conquering hardship, dream of Sundays fragrant with food. Take nothing from here, do not believe the rivers, the oceans. You can escape only upwards. It is not worthwhile to recollect upon the Earth.

Translated by Ottilie Mulzet

NIGHT JOURNEY

You write with two kinds of ink. One dries instantly: you can touch it,
read it. The other is invisible, like this city hidden
beneath recurring lamplights and smells, where you recklessly return,
invisible like the woman who awakens, sleeping unseen by your side.
What is invisible bursts abruptly from your senses, flowing everywhere
before you finish writing one sentence. What is visible follows blindly
the light-filled face. Write with eyes closed, as if you still had time.

The way of passion is dark. It's like the journey on a night train
which you do not take to arrive at another city, although
this is precisely your goal. Whoever boards a night train is building, unawares,
a palace for the moon, is crossing the lake-bottom's salt-lit waste,
his own desolate regions, weighing the possible and impossible, and only

the lights flickering through the window, the unread station names
signal that even unstirring, he is on his way somewhere.

In each instant, journeying cuts up space along a different line. Each place
is a station, threshold, entrance. But you are bound somewhere
with no threshold or entrance, where one can't stop, can't rest.
This is all you know for now. It will be the place of your belated birth,
where comparisons perish. You are preparing for another body that travels
along with you, as inseparable from you as the two sides of a leaf,
a mirror's transparent and silvered side.

Do not speak of temptation. The daytime fields have moved
to the mirrors' blind side: nowhere to see your reflection, and a view of faces,
a fiftyish man and a young blond woman, makes you fall briefly asleep.
You sit on a rocky beach, dark basalt columns towering above:
the water and columns arrayed not at your feet but above you,

multi-story, undulating. Nothing to be done: it's about to come crashing down.
Still, you tie your shoelaces and scamper like a madman toward the dark cliff wall.

You live in many bodies at once. Can thread, like pearls, the sequence of minutes
with no past or future, drink the milk of night until you choke,
but even if you travel far, you return: time measures itself
in your left-behind body. Minutes call for hours, hours for days,
days for years, as if you were tearing out basted stitches, arms reaching
into empty space, opening thighs, head turning, all breaking away from the torso:
the nights testify against you, your steps around the house a thief's traces.

If there were a brush to paint your face, it should paint you blind.
For long now you have seen with your body. The eye dwells there and in the eye,
desire calls you to life and death, to appear and vanish at once, splitting apart
your body: in vain women's scents, dew-like, alight on your skin,
you must be born from yourself. Draw your strength from the earth. If no one

can be nourished by two placentas, then let none nourish you, be your own desire, the earth that lets you in like a long-awaited lover.

The city where you return at dawn does not know the language of desire, of bliss, of things that change or flee, that shimmer disappearing. And yet you walk into the broad, palace-lined square like one come to recommence his time. How many dogged lies! For decades, attempts to tame imperial grandeur have failed here. Let not the triumphal arch erected for the lunatic procession admonish you to peace. Your war is only just beginning.
May your existence be pure trust and longing; in readiness, persevere!

[OM]

CAPTAIN CORNELIUS'S LETTER FROM PANNONIA TO BURRUS, TO THE COLONIAL OFFICE IN ROME

For you, a gently sloping, friendly country; to me, a land
of sluggish, nondescript winters, its climate unwholesome.
Only the thick wines offer consolation to the one who,
fed up with the ill-humored nepotism of governance
and, past his prime, realizes the odd pasquinade
is all his talent can yield.

And yet he goes on, hoping yet for autumn love, a bankruptcy
trusteeship, finding the pointlessness, here,
of making any change ever harder to bear.
Even though dying here in peacetime is no easier
than in any other province, and a reliable technique
of drainage was implemented over the centuries,

still, this frosty bog fringe was only livable
after the forgotten wars when they let
everything rot for a while, and the hyperactive ignoramuses
weren't bringing charges of mass murder,
imprisonment. Of course, all the wars were lost.
But not because they were unlucky.

They lost deliberately, and so they hoped
to cobble eternal forgiveness for themselves:
even today, they are entranced by funeral
marches and the ponderous fantasies of reburials,
their style, a mere parody, grows truly alarming.
So we took back this province. I find the fertile

heritage of local customs enchanting. I like
the colors of the houses, it reminds one of the closeness

of earth: dull browns and yellows succeed each
other, now and again a patch of mauve,
but the demands of grey are never resisted. No
attempt is made to fix the damages of time.

And yet, my good Burrus, what is this but deceit, ominous
deceit, for the land is theirs, it is their gods who lie
buried in the ground and whose names they no longer fear
to invoke. We should resign ourselves; we cannot correct
the course of time! All our spoils, apart from a few flocks
of sheep, is yet another unintelligible tongue, into which

it was a waste of time to translate Plato. Luckily
they are always the first to be scared off by blood.
And although after yesterday's assault, we may
expect more, for the moment all is quiet in this redundant

province. Let us hope the fatal infection will not spread from here. I am tormented by sinister premonitions.

Translated by Erika Mihálycsa

NOTE ON THE BACK OF A MAP

In memoriam Gizella Hervay

The house search lasted until dawn. Osip was arrested,
the warrant signed by Yagoda. Less than four years later,
Yagoda himself will be an NKVD prisoner, murdered first. Osip resided
in the Butyrka prison then. At night, when they transferred him
to the labor camp near Vladivostok, he was freezing,
he died there in December in unknown circumstances.
From there he will write: "In vain is poetry esteemed only in Russia.
There is no other country in the world where a person is murdered
because of it." In 1934, proceedings were halted against him,
thanks to his friends' interventions, but still not declared innocent,
he was sent into exile to Cherdyn. On the first night
he threw himself out of the too-low hospital window,
only breaking his collarbone, bruising his face.

He was obsessed by the idea they would come for him
at the designated time, carry out the secret
judgement. You were born the next day,
this too was a judgement. What a shame we cannot remember
tomorrow! "Here I lie, my face buried in death,
and I don't know why the death of tomorrow would be any different
than the death of today" — you wrote, and you were not wrong, because
when Osip lay beneath the hospital window, face bleeding,
collarbone broken, at the bottom of a freezing pit, like someone
who could count to three or four before the explosion, and
time became creased within him. So what street is this? —
he asked later, pointing at the map. It's your street,
answered a woman's voice. You see, there's nothing straight within it,
the whole thing is crooked. And Osip laughed as loudly
as he could. We should exchange heads, he said,
and you laughed too, you laughed until the Bucharest earthquake
that killed Kobak in 1977. But until then, the rains of eastern Europe

soaked many a poor soul through and through. Filth fell
from their mouths, rusty nails from their hair, brass buttons
of interchangeable faiths snapped off; the lipstick stains
of evenings past their warranty can never be erased.
History made its bed for underground love-making.
On that day when you stood in the draught of death, I became a man
according to the laws. Osip lives here with me now,
in a celestial sublet, you whispered. You both sit on the ladder's steps,
dangling your legs, look to see what you can see, listen to the silence
grazing below, steal the cowbells, giggle at everything
like schoolchildren. I saw how the ladder nearly broke
under Osip. The brew of the sky rumbled.
Since then, I walk the unknown streets like a thief. My brain
grinds out a line of poetry; you and Osip hang before me
from the last rooftops, like bats on the tips of eyelashes.

PREPARATION FOR THE CROWS' FEAST

We die here in a row, like little billy-goats.
Who praise the claw, hard labor, lying words,
happy to embrace the rosy flesh
beneath the spider-woven blanket. We are not silent

about the great secret. We don't glide for too long on time's crest.
After forty, a person's already a graveyard.
Gazing into the heavy rain, umbrella-covered faces,
we fancy grabbing some meat.

So we, like idiots, prepare for the crows' feast.
There will be weeping, cawing. If the victor marches by,
body bound to the cart, we might even laugh.
The great scam has been successful. We just don't know for whom.

EYES TURNED INSIDE OUT

Bigoted revenge cobbled together its Caesar once more. Indeed, nothing new
under the sun. Instead of the seven deadly sins, the silent demonstrators
held onto gloom the longest, and putting down their signs demanding a state of rights,
sneaked off, defeated, not daring to stir in the hostile crowd. They never did
regain their good companion, anger. Still, as of old, they keep laughing at themselves
when among friends. The one with the loudest whinny is an actor, recently diagnosed with lung cancer.

Open a book, point at a word! Try to combine its letters into
meaningful units. Consensus dictates what is meaningful. Come
to terms with yourself. Negotiate. Or gaze at the trams in the
September sun. The city has its moving mirrors carried around, the statues' eyes,
the same after two hundred years, don't grow old: life in the mirror
is youth's disease. But you want to be cured. Cured of the age,
unwilling to see how private and political pathologies overlap.

You carry two worlds within. Take long walks at night. You are like a ghost ship that keeps out of ports, though longing to berth, for one can only drop anchor in another's failings. Inside, you sail dark waters beneath dark skies. But your outward motivations are all the more shining. You're ready to fight where wars are merely suspended and where symbols, raving metaphors, murder without cease. Do so — be upright on the outside, at least. But don't think this is a way to your self.

One turns against one's self in shame and violent self-hatred when inner expectations cannot be fulfilled; self-respect vanishes. Words spoken at a tram stop by a poet gone silent for the past twenty years, the answer a comradely nod. Still, let's see what remains. It's raining, soon autumn will be here. Could our password be thumos? So that, shedding all wet things, halfway between anger and calm, we could at last become masters of ourselves, not begging for bravery's alms?

Your moods change with the moon. You experience but don't comprehend yourself. Or comprehend too many things at once, watch yourself with too many eyes while you should gaze like the Buddha: blindly, fixed on the brim-filled void. And still you set off? You don't know where to. How could anyone trust you? How could you trust yourself? Your very first step betrays you. You're like the midday moon. You walk unknown paths beyond your own self, where no one can follow. Prepare for the night! Look upon the Earth, eyes turned inside out!

There are no safe calculations. No path to the goal. When the amalgam of despair, wrath, and conceit is poisonous, the one who puts all his eggs in one basket may win. His victory brings a new set of rules. Those who speak his lingo like their native tongue are coming now. Keep clear of them! Walk in your sleeping city as if in a graveyard, so that time can befriend you. Draw courage from this: the city neither remembers nor forgets but its houses mold time, and it devours all its inhabitants in the end.

Like the Danube stretching out. Sign-posts half-submerged in the
water, stairs immersed, the benches where lovers and old folks used to sit,
no longer seen: there are such moments now. Count them — tear off the leaden helmet
that grew into your head, throw it far away. Get ready! Crack open the days
one by one like almonds, eat of them what was, what will be bitter, go to sleep each night
as if, in the morning, there could be a giant reindeer's head gazing through your window.

ATROPOS'S SCISSORS

A few rainy days in the middle of yellow-veiled,
Buddhist heat. The slide towards the equator
halts for a while. Demonic fever abates,
poison, released, washes away from the bodies.
The days have the names of cats again.
Only they, the cats, remember the patter
of the cobblestones, know how long the fig trees blossomed
below the castle, recall having recently batted at Turkish tassels
in the shade, finding a Jewish farthing in the grass, and why time
always passes without memories, backwards. Amazing
that some still believe in its ability to convey information.
The streets always lead to the same place,
for the hundredth time the curly-haired black girl steps out

of the newly built house, so that before Atropos
cuts the thread, for the hundred-and-first time, she fastens
her hair into an apple-shaped bun: enough change for now.
Wars were never taken seriously in this place. The first days
always seemed as if the age of eternal peace
were drawing near. Long tranquility can be redeemed
with one huge bloodletting, and the exiled king
will finally return. Doesn't matter if it's a two-horse landau
or a black Audi, or if the water system, the sewage pipes,
have undergone improvements, even today the poor
have the same sour stink. No one here ever had to learn
how to swim. Decades often fell away from
the calendars, and tomorrows demanded
the return of the dreamed-of past. So today we claim
the right to float, like bits of cork on the wine's surface,

slowly becoming drunk. On such rainy days as these,
we are grateful for the relief. The hatred within us subsides,
and although on the trams, the steam of humans
has not lessened, and the walls don't ever cool down:
perhaps we will succeed in politely removing the scissors
from Atropos's hand, and not begin to believe in providence.

YOUR SIRENS

"Gather up the accusations! Do not forget how much
the cold clatter of a tray will hurt when dropped
by the one whose attention you crave,
something like love. Do not forget how your face
turns to glass because of a delayed touch,
how quickly the indestructible towers of frigidity
build up within you. And do not forget fanatical
indifference! The ones who taught you to glimpse
darkness in the eyes of someone painting colors
upon the barren sky each spring; he enriches
the heart. Like a moldy old bottle, seal off
this darkness, for no one can be the womb that bore him.
The leaves in front of your window are stirring, you see,

but they make no noise. Like them, you find the shore
only inside." Sirens live there who wear cornflower-blue
skirts, scented silks, colorful blouses,
they whisper into your ears: "We are the men.
If you follow us, you will know our embrace, turning
first into a child, then into a woman." They are humming:
lingam, lingam, lingam. Their shore a wasteland, where
nothing ever grows. Still, you must follow them.
The passions that make you lonely must be returned
to their empire. Do not let not your faithfulness become
yet one more betrayal! Your sirens will imprison you,
until you stop calling. Their temptation leads you home.

WITH SILENT FLIGHT

It was not when they began to build the houses
on our mountains, houses higher than the crooked,
windblown trees, that the birds' cry of the heavens
went silent, and it wasn't when my throat
was crammed with fear, when it was time for the one
who had departed to give word of himself.

Something must have happened earlier,
when below, on the stony shore, there remained
nothing else of the dictionary of afternoon light, only myrtle
dripping with iodine, and here below, where everything
is much heavier, the air belonged
to the brisk pigeons. The most unassuming

of animals. Many say they are worse than rats,
although they are the last in which there is still enough courage,
enough trust to divide their existence in two parts: both to us
and to the sky, while, with their silent flight, they cleave apart
so much blue and white, for one single moment.

THE STREET'S INLET

The end of January. Last week, everything
was still frozen. But this morning, the first bird song
was heard from the trees one street over,
the row of façades, grazed with winter windows,
faintly received a little light.
Then, after a few minutes, algae-like darkness
settled in again. A trolley bus set off
jolting from its stop, carrying forgotten faces
behind grey glass windows. I turned towards them
and the street's inlet once again closed. The houses
watched with memoryless fish eyes, and whoever
stepped out of an entranceway was thrown back
in the next moment, as if felled by lead, sinking

into empty time. Maybe they saw me
that way too, I who looked at them. I came home,
ate something, and began to write. The end
of January. This morning, the first bird song
was heard from the trees one street over.

[OM]

CANVASES OF TIME

In the distance, the evening vapor's
dark mountains are silent.
Further below, immersed in gold,
stands the field of corn,

and where widened eyes are travelling
near the train tracks a few rows
of lettuce heads already dream
their mercury-hued

dreams. But on the canvases of time,
no sign awakens, no memory:
the great transformation of colours as yet

unknown. The dream of a moment beckons,

then runs away —

why is nonexistence so abundant?

[OM]

ABOVE THE GRAVEL PATH

I drink in troubled air like churning
dark water. Time is ploughed with numbers,
but there is neither good seed, nor aggregate, nor product,
no hand to cast the seed. If the earth
would be barren, it would be a golden care to cast away
burdens, to live the shortened hours, which I would
measure by the weight of observation and desire.

But chicory sprouts again for the mogul,
who sweeps away the colourful days, melts
milk-coloured lead into furious sunshine. Still,
he lacks confidence. His algebra is mistaken,
after division the remainder increases.

If more slate-years are to follow, and we will
have to study their scratchy writings,

then the moment will also arrive dressed in green.
Hungry waters fall before us, and above the gravel path
we sniff the fragrance of old songs.
Then we shall erase the blackboard. Our story
has not reached its zenith, there is time for germination.
We look again at springtime with puppy faces,
during the stolen evenings, time yet to wilt.

IN LIGHTNING'S FLARE

Only live in cities you can abandon at any time. Stay nowhere longer than seven years: before you leave, pay all your debts, paint the walls white. Take nothing as a keepsake. Not even something that fits in the palm of your hand. Even so, your body bears too many signs. You copied yourself in too dark eyes, they caress and scrape your skin. Eyes like knives. Before you leave, pick out one among them, put it where you are. See, observe — plunge it into your own self.

*

Sometimes you walk the streets like a madman. And you say you'd be more than happy to run out of the world, which only means that you are not where you should be, or that you are somewhere, when you should not be anywhere. Luckily, you meet up with an acquaintance. Before, you were still running breathless within; now flight subsides. And he speaks of the monotonous houses of Bern, the boons of polis-based Swiss democracy, community, personal freedom. No matter. For this day, you are saved.

*

You run in vain, but shall never, in one long sprint, vanquish all your spectres. Appease them one by one, venerate the one you can't
as a household god, for he prepares the future. Speak to him every day, ask for his help and counsel. Warm your palms in his presence,
as if by a fire. But if he speaks, do not believe a single word.
Around you laughter weaves a fine cord, until your phantoms, unpropitiated, burst into flames in your every sense.

*

Did you hear of the two soldiers lost in the Alps, already
in death's clutches, they wanted to give up, and one of them
found a map in his pocket? Gathering their remaining strength they set off,
followed the map, found the campsite again. Only then did they realize:
their map was of the Pyrenees, not the Alps. Does this mean
it doesn't matter which map you use? It doesn't matter whose skin you slip into,
just give yourself over as if you knew where you were going—to the infinite, the uncertain.

*

The moment comes when the streets close in: if you cannot strip away
the houses clutching at you, you'll be suffocated. Panicked, you sense
you're drowning, so forcefully there is no doubt: if you don't pack up
and get on the next train, you will die. And as the clutching sensation
eases a bit, do you believe yet again it was just a passing feeling,
and not the end of something? Do not retreat from the train's steps.
Remove your watchband from your wrist, throw it in between the tracks.

*

Every minute can become a lightning flare, leading to suffering, complaints, and fear
in the one who cannot birth himself, hoping for repetition and resurrection.
Don't play that tune. Where lightning touches down, the tissues are immediately charred, but
in that immeasurably brief moment before they perish, they send a message
to the brain: love the strength of fire! The brain does not decipher this message.
But on the skin of the forehead or below, on the nape of the neck,
a crimson spot appears as on newborns, known as the stork's pinch.

*

Separate your feelings from those of others, and from yourself as well. Take them
into your hands as if they were objects you can part from at any time,
and if you can't, if they don't let you, present them as offerings
to your unquiet demons. Until then, peruse them, know them well. Not with your eyes,
look with your fingers, with your fingertips, where the skin is even finer. It doesn't matter
what city the train sets you down in, it can even be the one from which you fled.
Live blindly, and within the lightning's flare, as if you have stepped across the wheel of time!

AFTER THE IRON AGE

Summer rebelled but had no rose, no march.
We wrapped ourselves in October rains: next to the road,
there were run-over dogs, spilt guts,
blood, hair. We talked in the car of marathoners
of unhappiness who, painting the green blossoms
of their three-year loves' skies nicotine yellow,
now sit with a beer can and an ashtray in old stuffed armchairs,
repeating, "Here at least we're home." Their eviscerated
loves first moved into the bridge's broken railings,
then into a picture, finally into the wall of an unwashed glass,
and when that broke too, the pieces were hurriedly
wiped away with a rag. We flee with shreds of summer
between our teeth, the weight of cobwebs

in our brains, but on the first mountain slope
a truck forces us into a queue. You can only catapult
out of here. Lost movements don't frighten
the shadows. Here, history is a disused industrial zone.
No one thinks of eternity after the iron age, ever faster
dissolving spectres are called in against madness.
The car rattles through an empty landscape. But the cobwebs
are still made of wire, and because the victim
never sees the execution, we still have nothing to say
about the death-grinding machinery.

[EM]

FAREWELL, RUSSIAN STYLE

To travel backwards, not omitting even
a single station. To gather all the small details,
erase them one by one from the train window,
like so much steam, empty pictures. To remove
the address from the envelope, empty the folders,
purge the computer's hard drive,

smash the telephone. Burn every note, sketch,
paper scrap, manuscript. Then, when everything is ready,
sit down for awhile, like the Russians, before departure.
Outside the basket is tied up, the light carriage, the heavy blanket on top,
the old horse harnessed. Be humble, proud man.
Then look one last time at the rooftops across the street.

In that view lay tranquility. To bid farewell to them,
rise from the chair, wash off the table and shelves
with much water. To leave this place so that no legible trace
shall remain. Thus may the true story of the road travelled
be preserved. Because nothing is ever taken back
by death, only changed. Once I underlined

this sentence in a book. Now I know:
this too is different. Death takes back
that which is lifeless, it does not change what lives:
a love stronger than my own existence inscribed the faces within me.
I give thanks that I could live with them, turning grey unto death.
Like smoke, like a summer cloud, so then it can disperse.

MARGIN

In the morning, here too
the scent of anise.

At noon: mirror-smooth
fanaticism.

The dry illumination
scorches all.

Now the slightest pressure, and
the walls will burst.

*

I sit by the window,
my back to the room.

The horizon is empty.

A seagull takes flight close
to the water.

The breeze has died down.
Today dusk
will fall early.

*

He cannot arrive from the
direction of the woods.

In the village,
dogs jump after him.

Disease-ridden and filthy,
like every other vagabond:

sewn into his mantle, he
carries the letters.

[OM]

TO MY DEAD

I cooked liver, placing it on a bed of lemon leaves
and fine spices, so its fragrance would entice you here,
my fleeing dead. Do you all know the death
of the heart, do you know thirst more torturous
and helpless than the desire of the landlocked for the sea?
And do you know the yellow decay that kneads the lungs
together like paper lanterns, hollowing out a wounded ditch
in the chest? More exhausted than the water-bearing
donkey, the camel with calf. Come, sit down
by the table, and while eating, look at the houses
scattered on the hillside, the sky, the cabbage
leaf, look at the plunging falcon, the women's
hips, the jugs set out on the windowsill, as if you were all

cut from living flesh, as if the kiss would never end, as if you could embrace all of this into one with the light, as if the world were nothing but pollution about to break free of God's embrace.

[OM]

PEBBLE

All of you who came to visit me,
who sat next to my bed,
or walked with me in the hospital garden

until I got too tired, and with cautious fear
in your eyes, told me to be strong,
that you have need of me,

to all of you, who were silenced by the news,
but you were thinking about me,
you were thinking of your friend,

and to you, my Lord, to whom
I have not been able to speak for so long, before my eyes
I lost the places of your refuge,

all of you should know,
that the course of days and nights
spent in various sick wards

amid breath's convulsions,
in pain, exhausted, broken,
that I spent in the nearness of death,

were beautiful, beautiful, beautiful:
as if I were clinging to the wall
of a forgotten temple,

and in pain, exhausted, broken,
I was submerged in a light with no flame,
but do not ask me what was there,

there was nothing I could show to you,
nothing worth more than a pebble
you have tossed into a lake,

I only know that after I arose,
as slowly my strength returned,
and I could move in the commotion of the days,

for a long time I wished again for the illness,
fearing that I had lost its gifts,
a lack remained for which there are no words.

GHOST HOMELAND

My ghost homeland, if I think of you, where shall I gather
enough love to swallow the repulsion regurgitated
from my stomach, the acidic bitter taste?
You never had morals, and while your grievances cast you
out from the world, your politics are murderous. Here in the heart,
like strings of Christmas lights, opiate lies glitter
and if the skies above you darken, by morning the obdurate
cretins, the slyly zealous, the patronizing malignant
will be ever more in number.

But, you see, even now I am awake. Behind me
is the bookshelf, full of volumes. What is it worth? I can no longer
mistake you for books. The rooftops opposite, beyond the windows,

extend into the distance, the street cannot be seen.
I hated going to school here. You instructed me early
in your injustices: the flame hardly blazes up
and the candle-snuffer strikes, it will be necessary to live
with less air, what is deserving does not come first,
hope walks with bent neck.

From the facades, gods with reptilian eyes
watch over every step. Who wishes to go home returns
to mute lands. And suddenly grows old, sitting
all day long in front of the softened screen, forgetting everything.
What did you raise me for, ghost homeland? Grey clouds
sit upon your cities, on the edges of maps, your starving children
scrape coal away from beneath cinders, yet you choose among the battered costumes
of a past century's bad finale? Is the aged chamber-waiter
still your favorite from the playbill?

The reptilian eyes' promise for tomorrow is war, perhaps.
If there is no hope, there is no fear, and what
is a neck vertebra compared to the night's darkness?
Terror, it is true, does not ease absence, from which
so much tedium and savagery ensue, but if you see
the refugees, will you again choose hanging
from lamps, the bridge, for them? Plaster-formed gods
never thought of eternity. This, after all, is terror's command:
may thought be concrete, like a kicked-out tooth!

This is the time of dreams, when instincts give themselves
over to aesthetics, and I wouldn't be surprised
if a sorrowful dromedary rested his head on my parquet floor,
asking if what they say about the needle's angle is true.
But the now lasts no longer than six seconds. As long as
time keeps narrating history, as long as it keeps eating

raw human flesh, it wriggles through its own noose. That is why the final means
of your prisoner, not wishing to kill, observing the ignominy
gathered upon your head, is the voluntary self-annihilation of flesh.

And so you enclose him all round with cordons, floodlights; torture him
with bellowing music, my ghost homeland? Is it because with a lucid mind
you can only be betrayed? The well-groomed delivery boy, smirking,
gets out of the official Audi, knowing that the trained denouncer,
the informer, when it is time to act, stops up his ears,
preferring to sit in the oily onion smell
and not open the window. Lest it should emerge
that outside is spring. Or winter, in which no snow
has fallen. Lest he should have to take someone's hand.

On the facades the traces of the old bullet-shots can still be seen.
Here wars only begin, and although the trains complete their routes

according to schedule, they never reach the end.
Every man on the platform knows his enemy, what
he'd gladly do to him. Whoever wants to reach another city
holds out in madness until the final cartridge. Do you know your shame,
my ghost homeland? Do you know why everything remains
in its place of ruin? The evening now is silent and pure,
sleeping within are those whose heart's beating is perturbed at noon.

[OM]

PREPARATIONS FOR A CITY

Is it possible to travel against a city? To return,
having decided beforehand: this time I cannot
allow it to burst open my foreignness, mortify me
with that immoderately direct gaze, as if knowing everything about me,
confusing my instincts and desires. It is possible to oppose repetition,
a city with a woman's gaze?

For there are gazes which, though led by curiosity,
not mistaken for touch, still bring the body to fever
chancing upon the soul's Achilles' heel. Gazes that do not want time
for themselves, but disturb and shatter with their memories.
Such gazes have no gender. They have it and they don't.
The gazes of women, too free; sharp, dissolving all resistance.

And if the moments split open, like iridescent bubbles
blown in all directions behind ochre-yellow wired glass, why does something
hover there in place of voice and countenance? Something which, luckily,
cannot be shown with a camera. Something which can only be forgotten —
no longer a voice, a face. It is forbidden to think upon it, even
to ask whose face that was. No one's.

Without sound, navigation lights blinking, an airliner, illuminated, ascends.
Flight as narcosis, clouds as desert, desert as ocean,
ocean as snow-covered plains. The body denuded of time,
the eye rests, the runway everywhere an unchanging
grey. I lean back, acceleration forcing me into the seat.
Preparation can never be completed. Gratitude for the dignified ascent.

Still, what gives rise to the need for repetition? Repetition of speech,
the most rigorous form of silence. Why is denial of complicity with the void

that remains after covered or buried passion not enough? And why does all this seem like retreat, as if I were sleeping in a conch-shell, burying myself alive? Though there is nothing, nothing in passion that can be termed as fate.

And if there were fate, who would not wish to evade it? Or is not life itself the evasion of fate? Fate, so easy to imagine into gazes, ornamenting them, clothing them with desire. Fate is the emptiness of heaven within us, which if released, its delirium opening but for a single moment, burns to ashes, annihilates all. Demented emptiness. Is it possible not to fall in love with fate?

Corridors lit by fluorescent lights, a row of closed doors. As if gigantic blocks of ice were behind them, cooling the city from below. Then stairs, elevators, lifting apparatuses. Bundles arrive on conveyor belts, continuing with impunity their discretionary routes. Breaking off like ice-blocks from the North Pole. Wind arises from somewhere, shattering a transparent automatic door into pieces.

A city approaches. Repetition is neither the plaything of time nor one of its deceptions, luring us into its mirror-covered chambers: showing one thousand faces, it takes that one face as well. Repetition is the eye of time, which gazes, instead of us, into one thousand mirrors, the emptiness of heaven within us. Repetition is the eye that sees the beginning. It hinders the plunge, as if grabbing the collar of a too-daring child.

And suddenly, the dread of space passes. Behind the opening automatic doors, the gleam of enamel, windshields, glass walls. Directions, broad and open. Air at last. Distance, which must be travelled alone, giving way to deeper passions. And yet so simple, like an etude. Ambling along the keyboard, with large pauses for breath. Finally, there is awakening — to awaken next to my beloved.

But until then I must persist in this foreignness, so that the pauses for breath may slowly lengthen, becoming crevices, then chasms in the city's body

where I run my route. Each building no more than two
distant voices tensing the silence like a chord, making it sound.
This is return, but not into the distressing known. A return to a living face,
a beginning always approaching from somewhere else.

PLUNGE

A fighter jet plunging, flames leap out.
Pitch-black smoke, deafening shrieks.
Eject! The command is for those who have
somewhere to go. Family? Europe?
The panic button's pressed, the brain breaks down the images
into their component parts. What do you see? Can you say?
No time for that now. Special neurons
analyze colors, shapes, contrasts.
You'll be out in a split second, as if

launched by rocket. Soon you'll know if the crash
is fatal, or if you stand a chance.
Consciousness perfectly sharp at last. The autopilot

receives ten million data per second, but only forty
are transmitted to you. Of course,
even so, you live in the past. You see
the ruined faces around you not with your eyes,
but with your memories, and like a surgeon, you sever
the hand that reaches out to you,

the smiles, unvoiced requests.
Destruction is all you're good for. You deny
to yourself, without pain: cannibalism is not the
mere preserve of the past. Since birth,
you've been swallowing the filth of a hate-ridden beggar nation.
That's no excuse. But whatever happens,
there'll always be something else, and illusions
are no exceptions. If, on leaps days only,

you head down the street, sending messages
and emails, then cooking refined dinners
with unusual spices for your children, your wife,
maybe some friends, all this can be forgotten
for a while. The brain knows what is important,
keeping for itself what is familiar.
It self-alleviates, cools down. Even now
it can't decide if what is going on in the street
is a murder, or a savage mating ritual.

In the meantime, there is news of a teacher,
who, along the uncertain borders, took drunken
hooligans to his old school to attack
six-year-old Roma kids, and a gangly teen
texts a friend from the tram: Hurry up, shithead.
Every experience leaves its trace in the brain,

and can be called up from the archive at any time,
if linked to some emotion. You would, of course,
be happy to unlearn this language. But the next

moment this, too, turns into ammunition, an argument
against yourself and the country—anyone past forty
is a perfect sleepwalker, the private
and collective imagination in him
can no longer be unraveled. And so the autopilot's signal
always flashes too late. The crash
is unavoidable. What kind of hope did you want?
How lucky the brain is a born atheist,
for one can depart only in the brain.

DIAGRAMS IN THE RIVER

as the rings of the traces of two oars
entwine around each other in the water, for a moment
the form of the number eight is clearly seen,
then the ripples become blurred.
perhaps there is a kind of distance from which
endless birth and disappearance may be
precisely observed, if the boats proceed
in one direction, and neither one is quicker,
or slower, than the other. but
do two such boats in reality exist?
infinity is the simultaneous, accidental
beating of two oars, and if there is a pair of eyes
that can read the diagrams of the river, that too
is precisely such a gaze, inadvertently opening.

HUNGARY, ETERNAL ELLIPSIS

Hungary, you eternal ellipsis,
assignment handed in blank,
weed-choked cemetery, beggar's alms-box,
a job for a maker of maps!

You blood, you soil, memory of horror,
bellowing drunken monster,
wretched ghost-image on our screens,
if I call out, you're not even there!

Not even there, if someone declaimed you
which could last only for one minute.
The child's bed a catafalque yet again,
your sad cretinized son, look upon him!

Not even there, even if someone still lived here,
beyond all hope, yet granting you trust,
until you devour all of his cells, you on the x‑ray,
you, the spreading dark splotch.

Hungary, you eternal ellipsis,
above you the scrawl of time's weary hand!
Forget the map, the coin's tossed, it's heads,
Time for your fogweed November to end!

[OM]

DAWN LIGHT

The crying of an infant heard through the window.
Cool dawn light sails across the yellow wall
of the house. The gaunt song, the late arrival,
lays the table again with the thick homespun
of generations, begins to enumerate
the forgotten names of birds. The street
does not pay attention. The houses know the prediction
of the great rains, of lightning bolts.
In this winged cemetery, even the newborn
does not tire. The crying from his thrush-sized lungs,
between the window frames, beyond the rooftops,
still ascends. We have no faith
in the unknown. We would flee from it, but only

if we can tie the rope ever tighter
within ourselves. Who could open
those aching bluish eyelids, as if awakening
from a dream of seeing the dead? Who will give
eyes to the dawn light? If we were to know
the true equation between wings and darkness,
we would not have to take hope
from the crying of the newly born. But at this
algebraic feast, often falling into despair,
can we imagine another time?

[OM]

THE TASTE OF SALT

It would be enough if a mug fell off the table.
Enough, if a gadget broke down, if I spilled
soup on my shirt. Enough, if one of us
didn't hear a sentence's end. A missed phone call
would be enough, a twitching of the face not revealing
what you or I believe. It would be enough if you or I
still hoped for something. Enough, if we forgot to remember,
if we both tried to imagine how things
could be good, or at least better than they are now.

It's better than it used to be. When we looked out from the window
at the chestnut tree's green globe. Now the leaves
are rust-colored, the sap dried up. The designated times

are islands with no crossings: comparisons
take the place of traffic. The chestnut tree used to change colors
every day; every day the sap drained from the leaves.
But we didn't notice. We inhabit islands: yesterday we lived on one,
today on another. It would be enough if one of us
were fed up with these endless comparisons.

If one of us could believe that time is a sea and that, under water,
our eyes closed, we could grasp tomorrow's fin.
That someplace, some promontory exists, from where, looking
up and down, everything is bathed in the same blue. For it is hardest
to be here, where we are. In this skin. To be in this
eternally arid, half-completed otherworld. To be where
we are needed, or maybe not, where we could
remain only if we could stop making love,
if we weren't nailed down to the absence gaping within.

Comparisons are like a sickness you can't
get rid of. They nestle in your system, vanish
for a while, then flare up again. The eye is inflamed,
because it wants to see. In self-protection, it begins to
tear. And tears remind you of the sea again, of a journey,
of vast salt ponds stretching for kilometers
along the shore. Their water is not blue like the sea,
but brownish. The eye is one such pond. If time evaporates from it,
fever's white crystals remain on the bottom.

But it is not for us to collect the salt. The one who will
compare two things, who in restlessness counts beyond
one, will never be able to stay in his skin. No matter what
he says or does, he tries to rush ahead to extremes but can't,
for no one can shed his skin. The fires light up in his body here and there.

It takes less than a casual word: the cause, if there must be one,
will be a word or gesture that failed to happen.
If absence turns stifling in a repressed system,
autoinflammation is likely to start in the cells.

The body's habitual self-cooling mechanisms will not
help at such times. Walls burn through, and what, in the body,
we term the soul, is torn to pieces. The only external signs
are the red spots on the neck and chest; the skin
becomes marble-like. Inside, though, the most malevolent thoughts
traverse the brain. You ponder the death
of the ones you love. Body and soul function in death mode.
No telling how much time passes. Although, right now,
nothing matters more. Inside, everything darkens,

becomes ever darker. The sediment on the bottom of the pond
is still invisible; above, the water is the color of mud. Someone
still lies there, outside. Not knowing what to do. Horrified timelessness.
And then not he, but someone else within him, begins to pray. Asks for a new body.
For a new soul, in a body, whatever it might be. He can't get to the end of the words,
and isn't sure he'd like to. But this seems to be enough.
His forehead and back are drenched in sweat: cold, unsalted.
And the soul pretends it has nothing to do with all this.
It merely wanted to discover the taste of salt.

[EM]

INVISIBLE WAR

Glints of the tram. The nondescript houses
dream numb underwater dreams. Faces are
transparent bubbles popping off from the windows
where water used to break through. The pedestrians
crossing to the other side of the street drag
heavy years in their shopping bags. Better to forget
them. Some ended up on the hook
of a quick death. Some merely fell ill
and when they healed, let ivy run over the balcony
railings and grew flowers in a case. While
continuing to write, on and off, less and less.
The screech of brakes can't wake you now from sleep.
Cartilage calcifies, an uninhabitable archipelago

sediments on the frontal lobe. And nothing
can dull the metronome beats of fear.
The tram gets stuck on an octagonal square.
The passengers scream and bang the doors.
No help in sight. They're slowly overgrown by
the tracery of the centuries, small anthozoa.

NOVEMBER

Like the numbing November fog, enclosing
bridges, houses, rivers into sheaths,
it breathes and thickens, in its arm's-length
infinity my face, cold as a statue, is lost,

that's how dispirited I feel now.
I breathe and I move. But while my hand gropes
for some kind of tangible object,
the houses and river disappear,

and as I step towards the railing of the bridge,
from arm's-length infinity, hands are
stretching out to me. I reach them,
and below, into the fog, my face disperses.

GRAVEL AND REEDS

Will nothing now ever break
the evening's cast weight?
I am prisoner of a cry
that can't get out of my throat.
My breath is gravel and reeds.
Unknown spirits reside in my word-castles,
as in the windswept world, where
no living heart ever arrives.
Winding amid spinning desires,
giving birth to oneself, motherless, stuck
in the birth canal. But while from darkness
wave breaks upon wave thick and grey,
stabbing between my ribs with every intake of breath,

at last I begin to see myself. There is no other hope
than for despondent suffixes
to penetrate the bones, to attain
the wakeful nights within: the body
lying chilled on the operating table.

[OM]

OFFERING TO DEATH

Packing separates, protects, hides.
Packing is indifferent and vulgar.
To pack up, to conceal what never was, never will be,
only important to someone no longer important.

Let packing be commonplace, imperceptible.
For the chest, shoulder, stomach, there's the shirt.
The thigh, legs, and groin
squeezed into the channels of the trousers.

What's a foot worth?
Hands are protected by gloves, necks by scarves.
And for a face? What should there be for a face
whose eyes, whose mouth betray everything?

The eye has no radius.
The face, like Galvani's frog-leg,
twitches once. The mouth opens,
babbles something incomprehensible.

Surely still alive. Then the rectoscopy
can be administered. To reach the section
to be examined, the site of the operation,
all the way up to the sharp bends.

The hand, the waist, and the ankles are being drained.
The bed, surface of agony,
comes to an end in bars and a circle.
Now there's yelling too. Where the voice comes from,

where the surface is being lifted, is the head.
Wrap it up in tinfoil!
Wind the silvery foil all around, to the point of suffocation.
The eyes, the mouth, into silver foil.

Then slowly flip the bed over.
The body hangs by the straps, ready to plunge.
The visible surface is empty and clean.
Present your offering to death.

FROM BENEATH THE LETTERS

I shall remain in that place where I never was.
Beneath the tent of sightless evenings
I dug out the star of your body,
now I bury it with letters.

The impetus of desire shall
be restrained by reality.
May a thousand games of mirrors pass
us to each other,
so that we disappear from each other's sight,

so that light will be cast from the star of your body,
from beneath the letters, where you never shall reach.

THIRD DAY UNCEASINGLY

All of those worn-out,
good-for-nothing objects,
the two rusty pruning shears,
the torn jute bag, spade handle,
wooden ladder, the spilled-out sands
now turned to stone, the nails
and the saw, snake of green plastic,
the wading pool's hole-punctured wall,
yes, that too, although afterward
it was really good for nothing,
and all those useless pictures,
as we idiotically scrambled for an umbrella,
caught by the winter storm

on the road that led to the sea,
the wheatfields of Umbria,
and the tram, clattering, that stopped
before the confectioner's, and started off
again like a heavyweight boxer struggling
to his feet after being knocked down,
and that decaying wooden bridge —
we trotted beneath it in rubber boots —
raindrops like pearl-strings bursting apart,
I should have taken care of all these things,
and for them too, for my dead:
Magda, Péter, Szilárd, my father,
I don't understand why they're not sitting
with me now here in the kitchen,
why they're not asking me for a glass of water,

I should have been taking care
of their voices, the warmth of their hands,
making sure the doors were closed after they left:
I should have built them a house,
a house for all those worn-out,
good-for-nothing items,
for all those pictures
that will not be battered by the wind,
nor torn by the snow,
the sun will not scorch
nor oblivion bury them,
and they will not stand around solitary,
out there outside, stamping their feet,
for the third day while it unceasingly rains.

THE STAR OF TIME

Dawn, from its enormous flagons, spills mist
everywhere. A thick cloud looms,
yellow light of nothing. On the walls of houses
are the damp posters of yesterday's elections.
Empty faces, calculated fear.
Maple trees by the road, leaves turning brown,
the fog hangs down from them like bags
amid the cars' roaring. Scholars have been
writing poetry for a long time now. They observe
the collision of two neutron stars, measure the waves
of gravity. But who hears the echoes of crude
wild laughter, of fog-mouthed time? Like an ice
skater closing his eyes, arms pulled in,
its star spins ever more maniacally.

SINKING ISLAND

A ballroom above the arched entranceway,
built for clamorous conflicts. Shipwrecks
in the mirrors, as in a mother's womb.
From branched chandeliers, from crystal
light fixtures, hang dead poets,
on the soles of their feet, the sinking island.
Yellow paper-faces, the language cooled down long ago.
The new law condemns everyone of insufficient faith
to labor camps, because our enemies
are truly evil, a mere speck of doubt could cause
our beloved homeland to fall into their hands.
Down below, from marble-white necks,
on blown-off heads, balance

the hats of bird-murderers. A few fusillades
ring out, someone calls out the year,
jubilation on the cobblestoned street.
Let our enemies tremble in trepidation!
For our brains are not slumbering ivy,
but hardened boxing gloves. We crash
through the white double-winged doors,
our silhouettes, garbed in women's clothes,
tear apart the barbarians conjured
there. And the island finally sinks.

[OM]

DUST

The letters I write down fly away like dust.
Not to the sky, but into the void, just as
the dead keep stepping forward there as well.
Only alive for as long as I keep stumbling on for them.
Some idiotic instinct must be the reason, the same
that explains why women give birth to them, the dead. Until then,
my ankles, my knees, my hands, will keep fracturing for them. It is for
this stumbling that I returned from the courtyard of death.
That is why every day, I sew my manifold disguises once
again. No kind of eye can see me — I know truly
I am invisible, like a bald,
naked woman. I make my way on legs that have grown
from fear, legs that fracture with every step.

These legs will not carry me for long, and only now have the meaning of the movements, the words begun to open up before me. I don't even know what I was doing until now.

[OM]

NIGHT OF FORESTS

Before the mirror, that cursed mirror
where my grandmother combed her hair,
she combed eternal November,
she combed the fog that wouldn't pass,
the burning shed, the forgotten names,
she combed her hair until it fell out
to the very last strand, now it is me
who stands before the mirror, I get undressed,
take off my sodden clothes, as they did too, before
they stepped into the tin cans,
in they stepped, and I ran away from Poland,
I wanted no diaries, memories, no atonement machine,
because there is no word to cleave myself in two,

and even now I have no wish to traverse the night,
the door is open, it hasn't closed for a long time,
toward the hillside there is no kind of fence,
naked, I wait —
come now, Polish forests,
light a fire in my grandmother's mirror,
the wolf's fur is blazing crimson,
let them howl, be burnt to ashes,
I still know the prayer scratched out from beneath the pillow:
blessed be the night of forests,
blessed the chasm of the mornings,
may every unfinished day be blessed,
only that road which is the traveler's death,
I want,
I want,
I disappear without a trace.

AGAINST PHANTOMS

If there were counsel against phantoms.
if a swish of the cane could silence
the echoes bringing trouble, then
you would not find a path across this dark domain,

you would not be able to live in your city
where every night, the houses are beaten
with iron rods. As your own
phantoms are released, bubbling from

each other, evoking pain and
crazed anger, so you will emerge
from your self of tomorrow. Let tranquility
ripen within you instead of anger.

You disappear without a trace. For if the goat knew the danger, would it run away from the wolf, would the lion's howl evoke terror in the sheep?

[OM]

IT WILL SHINE

The fabric of the darkened streets has shut down.
We believed we were kissing the heart of the age,
but the snow of our love, in one week,
became sullied, disappeared.

It's January, with a fatal peace.
On the street corner, a beggar's black-clothed
back disappears, the greengrocer runs out of the shop,
looks to see if anything was stolen.

He inhales the breath of the grey sky
into himself. The clump of lime in his veins
hardens. Should he sleep another
thirty years, until the epoch opens

its tired eyes? And until then?
At dawn, salt, instead of snow,
will be scattered on the pavement.
It will shine like conscience.

[OM]

AMOUNT OF EARTH

Your demons are silent and motionless. You cannot speak to them
as if you were talking to yourself. You suffer
instead of them, feel your happiness awakening. They live
within you, like a child in an adult's body, his entire story
carried within his bones, and yet barren, not wanting
anything not of himself. The enemy of your demons is the earth
which, even dead, even arid, can yield. Search within yourself
for the earth, and if you find it, place a plant in a clay pot
as a memento. Then at last
you can trim your beard, grown out for weeks.

Do you think you deserve more than others
from those daily, weekly rations measured out on this thin,

crumbling edge, this unknown land where we drag
along our sacks and guts? The less water and bread
there is, the more you demand. You find someone
who gives it to you, your self-forgiveness comes easily.
You awaken with impunity, you lie down
with impunity. You are forgetful. Today again at dawn,
you started awake, afraid. You began to implore the one who lives within you:
may the rattled-off months not obviate your impunity.

Earth's deepest point is dead. The human body hovers
on the saltwater's surface. Death also has its living creatures.
Divers have found, thirty meters deep, freshwater springs;
in chimney flues enormous microbe colonies
are living. Everything begins anew with them.
The microorganisms synthesize themselves
as carbon molecules, creating crimson

fluorescence in lakes. Previously, such lifeforms were found
only in incandescent, anoxygenic surroundings. The microbes shine
like tiny lanterns beneath the electron microscopes' lenses.

In the end, how many souls do you want? Why can't you stand
on one leg like a tin soldier, or a stork?
Why does it always have to be someone else who gives their leg
so you can stand, their arm so you can reach the unattainable,
their lap so you can feel like an adult, and they think of you
instead of themselves? Someone who always
has time for you, whenever you want, then unneeded,
disappears without reproach. Someone who gives
you their most severe words so you will chew,
digest, and chew them again.

The amount of earth that fits in a clay pot is exactly enough
for you to have something in common with the daytime. Observe,

irrigate the bends in the road. Go out onto the street,
remember the war that ended yesterday, although
tomorrow it will break out again. Remember the watchwords,
the epistles of the nameless. By the time you walk to the end
of the street, it will always be evening, October darkness. Why does time bother
with these changes? Here, only besmirched objects aroused
its sympathy, history was never anything else than the horrified
gnawing of mouthfuls, spit out and re-swallowed.

Still, did you wish for a strength to tear you suddenly away,
turn you out of yourself, subtract you from your bonds,
unlock your strength, without you having to do anything,
as if a bird of prey had snatched you, transporting
you to a higher cornerstone? Your despairing hopes
trickled out of you like urine
from a hanged man. You were too weak to climb the steps.

It wasn't the tower you wished to attain, but its peak.
And because everything around you seemed to shrivel,
you thought your downtrodden heels raised you high.

Your demons tell you that war is the mother
of all things. You will have to hear the stories
told about you, only afterwards will you be able to ask.
You will find out if you are lucky that in the midst of their fury
not every one of your bonds broke, or if it would have been better
to seize a knife. Because life always begins
with a volcano eruption, then the images calm down.
Children armed with pistols break into a movie theatre,
cobblestones, Molotov cocktails are flying. Here inside,
it is still dark. Alone, you stare at your own forgotten self.

SUMMER RAIN, TRANSPARENT BORDERS

Skin — the blood vessel's wall — is translucent. The borders
within are invisible, just as they are without,
in that city of genial incongruity. That is why
you are an eternal violator of borders. You would build the city
outward from within, would never know where you walk.
You'd always be in at least two places at once. You'd research directions
without fear, question stranger's eyes,
wanting their tomorrows. Leading to the liberation
of overly excessive strengths. You build, within days, entire boulevards,
streets where no one could ever live.
You leave behind yourself innumerable monuments
to imagination and desire, deceive others and yourself,
and it is to be feared that your only true deed,
standing before you now, is destruction.

*

The city is built by oblivion. Chocolate-brown dogs
run in the parks either on the left or right side of the Danube.
Barges transport the darkness. The parks
are fenced in, and in springtime new flowers are planted,
forget-me-nots, pansies. From time to time, statues
are pulled down, new ones put in their place, the streets
are given new names, but are called by the old ones long afterward.
And inexplicable changes occur. From one day
to the next, the sparrows disappear. The chess players
vanish from beside the stone tables in the park.
Words and sentences are erased from books.
No one remembers that they used to be there, and if a few return,
everyone is astonished, and no one understands them.

*

The strength of ruin seethes in the chasm of longing for love. Precipice dark and deep, it devours every smile, every touch, destroys every light penetrating within. And yet an eye may illuminate its damp walls, cause the specks of dust floating in the dark to burst into flame: these will be your stars. For there is no measure of this emptiness which, were it to step into the world, would cause every tree to bear fruit, and yet devour everything, strangling within itself everything that was separate. What kind of lack in the world becomes, within you, so hungry — what is not, nor ever was of the world that must be replaced with words, touch, embraces, kisses? With every step, you are moving both here and in an absence-world.

*

On a neighboring plot of land, there once stood a small textile factory.
A one-story building, from the time when there
were no apartment buildings here. Later on,
as the street was built up from the boulevard, the other factories
moved further north, but the small textile factory
remained, closed, empty. I liked to stand
in front of it. Before its construction, this district
was a single unbroken swamp which had to be filled.
A few years back the factory was also demolished.
A bulldozer arrived: by evening, the walls were gone.
Now a new apartment building stands there,
completely different than the old ones. Was this demolition
or construction? Does the city know these words?

*

Now the borders are drawn by heat. It slows down
the bodies, burnishes, separates them.
The numbness in the muscles does not slacken for a long time.
And you incline yourself to the one who opens
their door to you, for your body retains the soul
of an eternal child, you are incapable of giving birth to yourself.
The moments roll around in front of you like peas.
That is why there is a lack in you that cannot be replenished,
just as the one you embrace in vain is lacking from you,
the hour passes, once again you hold out the chasm of your own self to the other,
wounded, accusing. But do not fear, the next moment
will again be overflowing. You must only wait,
just as the walls wait for rain.

*

You acquired your first experience of transparent surfaces
when you were three years old. You stepped across
a freshly cleaned glass door. The almond-shaped scar
is still there above your right knee. It would have been enough
for you to look to realize: the crossing of borders is always invisible,
always accompanied by blood. Now is the time to cut open
the wound with a glass shard. The blood has eyes,
look with those! Realize what shadows were always
coming right after you, what fierce robbers.
What held them back, what did they take? What did they repulse
you towards? Get to know the coward within them, the merchant
of darkness, yourself. Have you scrubbed a single moment as clean
as water's surface, thinking back on how easily you could break through it?

*

The greatest incongruity is that you are here. When none
least expect it, drops of rain begin to patter
on the tiled roofs. Down below, the cars rumble
one octave lower, from the boulevard
comes the clatter of trams. The city's asthmatic breathing
is in no way eased. The summer rain quickly passes through,
the air is filled with vaporous heat, the clouds swim like swans
above the roofs. Watch carefully, because not a single swan feather
can be lost until the tempest beyond time breaks out.
Would this be the enchanted dark lake? For how long will you try to escape
your own shadows? Your life, either way, is a lying fairytale,
and it's good if a tiny remnant, like a puddle,
remains below. Time to put a full stop.
But how to put a full stop on the water's surface?

[OM]

IN THE JEWISH CEMETERY IN WORMS

The emperor's cathedral rises triumphantly
above the slanting gravestones. The ones who
paid for royal benevolence in gold and cast
cinders onto the rooftops of the ghetto only
in times of plague found tranquility in non-
existence. When young Rashi came to Worms
from Troyes, a rabbi posed a riddle to him at
the Sabbath table: what is there where it may
not be, for it belongs elsewhere, there where
it always was, and it shall never be there ever
again. Rashi laughed all that evening, and the
next day when the moon came out anew he
answered: a new Jerusalem may be built from

the gravestones, but then came the time when the graves were dug in the air, and the four letters disappeared: a great miracle took place there. The blackened Torah is now an object on display, the gate named after Rashi the Wise and the cameras film the air.

DOUBLE INUNDATIONS

The happy hours pass quickly, the bitter ones
slowly. Still, they are the same. The green of the
trees throbs, in a circle, along the inner horizon. Then
in the evening, the heart fearfully, in anxiety

or courage, perhaps with ease, measures out its
own time. The bed is transformed into a light,
swaying boat, tilling the waters of dream and
wakefulness. Only with difficulty does the soul

give itself over to the uniform rhythm of double
inundations. A desire always remains within
that resists; the thrusts always coming from in front

or sideways. How can it be satisfied with just one life? Every moment is only preparation, with neither goal nor beginning.

THE COLOR OF PAIN

Swelling walls, staircases leading nowhere,
winding back into themselves, blinding pulse. Nothing exists,
only what is within the body. Focal points, radiation,
migration. Strengthening, then momentary abatement.
What I am grows denser in pain. In that point, where.
Not more distant, not on the other side, not farther away. Here, and here.
I point to it, even if there isn't anyone around. For long now the routes
have lead into its impossible darkness. Every feeling turns within, inscribing
dense curves, registers. No certainty, no home front.
Eyes closed, I draw the wires along which the messengers
of pain run. You will suffer much before you die.
And beg for a hastier death. At the highest point,
where sounds break off, the spotted back and neck
of a cat comes into view, then disappears.

THE CARDINAL DIRECTIONS

Why do we run away from each other? Here, every evening
could be spent beneath four lampshades. We venerate the cardinal directions
with them. We have no compass. Neither instinct,
the heart, nor reason write the rules for us.
That is why we need light: blindness is creeping into our eyes.

If the thread breaks in the glass bubbles, and the socket
turns coal-black, we still don't hurry to change the
bulbs. Whoever chases after his own self within,
addressing dark shadows, soon comes to love
the semi-darkness, does not hasten for substitutions.

He doesn't believe every mirror-eye he comes upon.
Frequently turns back the pages of the calendar.
Now it is March, recently snow fell. At noon, behind the windows,
skin grows heated. The map of the branches and twigs
is like that of the streets. The city does not release its sleepers.

The fresh data is downloaded in the morning: who steps out
of the entranceway is captivated by faces' illuminous deceptions.
He observes hungrily, copying every bodily message,
by evening nothing remains, only the white hand
bidding farewell, the smile vibrating on the screen.

And what we do conceal from ourselves, what do we not see
in this continual disquiet, making no noise around us,
if darkness falls, binding us to ourselves,

to each other? That no one will be born from us anymore; if we look back, no one will follow in our traces.

[OM]

UNDER THE BAT'S WING

Dawn banished nighttime with lights, rumbling,
and with it every promise. From the city, streets disappeared,
staircases vanished from houses. The people
now walk on ledges, throwing planks
across ever narrowing gaps, lower themselves
on thick ropes, ascending again with skillful hoists.
How many years have we slept under the bat's wing!
We hunched together, away from searching lights,
but heard murderous whispers from the cracks.
Now all around us, the walls reverberate and rumble.
The light explodes, the pillow is aflame, the quilt, the bedsheet.
Two bodies, caressing each other, their wings already
torn off, guard the night. Outside, cameras

pan the scene, hooks, clasps, pulleys are sliding,
further on a crane lifts heavy wooden chests from a house's
stomach. There is no entrance, and I don't know
how to be saved from fear, annihilated by the world.

[OM]

GREETINGS FROM THE INTERIOR OF THE CONTINENT

The last local train creakingly stops
on the outermost tracks. The spirits take back
their wearied, dark bodies and step onto the damp platform,
whoever has an umbrella constructs a bunker
for themselves in the drizzling rain, glances towards
the closed kiosks, prepares for the first attack.
The city closes its eyes, unobservant of ruinous
intentions. It lives ever more noisily, renouncing sickly
hopefulness, wishing, both day and night, only to eat.

Where the food is good, time can be turned back
thirty years. Once again, restaurants are the hiding-places
of the aggrieved. The tablecloths are checkered, the door creaks,

salt and pepper shakers, toothpicks are set out on the table,
but smoking is prohibited. Still, it is better
to wait outside for the pogroms' uniform apparitions.
In the city's outskirts, the roots of weeds drill
through the cement, but on the boulevards the trams run
even after midnight, and murderers no longer

escape with ambulances. So there is reason for calm.
Whatever happens, the music of the rail tracks never changes,
the rain beats down only on those with no bed.
And on the flowers on the monument's plinth. No one can rip the sword
from the bronze bird's claws. The law of time is like that
of the winds: it doesn't matter from where, just keep on running.
If you send a postcard from here, don't write anything else. Do not betray
the name of the city. We can stick it out till morning in the bunkers.
Outside, cement slabs shine in the neon light.

TRENCH

When a new patient walks into the sick ward,
everyone can tell what stage he's at.
The beginners still have their hair
and eyebrows. They are terrified. Not understanding
why fate has brought them here.
When someone arrives for the second or third time,
completely bald, they take out
their slippers, their toothbrush cup,
as if finally coming home after
a long journey. They go to the toilet, whether hopeful
or not. Don't make a big deal if they have to vomit.
Or get bad results. If someone is here
for several months, and after brief improvement

their condition worsens, the malignancy
growing in the stomach, or a new tumor found
behind the forehead, then they show you
where it is, no more strength
for fear or hopefulness.
No demand for any particular attention
for themselves. The nurses treat them
as if they were a piece of furniture,
old and beloved, but ready to be scrapped.
The last infusion is administered, no one asks
if there were bowel movements.

Each body is distinct. But like
soldiers in the trenches, legs
numbed, they belong together.

COME BACK

On her chest, where they operated,
a picture was tattooed.
An angel descended to its inverted sky,
outside it snowed.

Pushing the stone away, the angel
sat at the entrance to the cave.
It sank into the skew-eyed
evening light: good thing it never gave birth.

Six months after the first operation
her stomach was cut open too. What the chemo
left in the veins, the aorta,
they took out the lymphoma.

It was cold in the operating room. She froze.
Into her, a needle injected a dream.
The last thing she saw was a hand
as she fell into a narrow sheath,

filled with egg-like light.
The angel waited in the corridor.
Group photographs of doctors on the walls. A nurse
at times clattered across the sick ward.

Hours went by like this. Awakening in intensive care.
Her stomach sliced open to the sternum.
You are beautiful, beautiful, the female likeness of my body,
veiled in nothingness's palm.

And the angel leaned above her.
In her ear, it whispered:
Adonai, Elohim, Sabaoth.
Come back to the cave-night.

[OM]

FEAR

I dreamt about you for the first time since your death.
You sat in an armchair, your face emaciated,
dejected, gaunt. You did not resemble yourself
when alive, but I knew that it was you.
I touched your shoulder, you didn't even tremble.
You did not address me. I wouldn't refer to this
as a meeting. When you were alive, our language
was silence, but the silence you left behind
is full of apparitions of decease. If we could talk,
I would ask you about fear. The fear which slipped
into me after your death, its harvest
a series of nut-sized swellings.

BEYOND THE OPEN WINDOW

The clocks were set back. Some set their watches
back by twenty years, some by forty.
Ask them, for they will know the exact time.
If this were the central station, where everything runs
by predetermined schedule, the deceptive trains,

although late, would finally arrive,
and the clock, unreachable in its height, would show
neither minute nor hour hands. But here below, order
and calculation falter. You tore the hands off your watch
long ago. Asphyxiated, you were always

the mountain-climber of instants — so you should
remain. And just as a climber's every muscle
embraces an entire mountain,
even when sliding, plunging to the depths
along the icy slope, so now do you sit by

the opened window. Go on your way to the dormant
evening, to the grey-green rain, to whatever comes along,
as if, clinging hopelessly to your darknesses,
you could stop the falling. Count
the cold drops beating down on your face.

[OM]

SHEATH

A summer's night, dense thunderstorms. The sky lights up
above the Country of Phantoms. There is no road, but there is direction.
The windshield-wiper swings back and forth wildly like a scarecrow's
sleeves. Two people sit in the car. They don't speak to each other,
the woman drives. In front is the headlights' uncertain,
narrow halo, surrounded by night's drenched, thick-woven
draperies. No eyes were ever sharp enough for this bird-barren
land. The red phosphorescent stripes on the roadside posts
are illuminated too late. The woman drives slowly.
Her knuckles on the steering wheel are white. All that is real
is ringed by the body of the car and the windshield.
Their gaze must rip apart this sheath.

The man looks to the side. The lightning flashes
ever closer, no pauses now between the claps of thunder. He looks back.
Are their feelings truly replicas? The woman is afraid. An oncoming car's
lights blind them both for a moment. The windshield-wiper clatters;
something in the engine makes a knocking sound.
They approach the heart of the Country of Phantoms.

NEW CENTURY

In memory of Osip Mandelstam

We are living, while the country sinks
beneath our feet. Its illusory lawns sway.
Does the spine of two centuries yet cling
with mire and blood? The depths of lake weed,
water lilies cast up the devoured beast, its eye sockets
stare at us. To step into a new day—
what the new century desired. Already it shudders,
seeing what kind of birth this is.

The beast's spinal column
is not made of delicate cartilage.
It's ramshackle, dead, calcareous.

But it betrays how much strength its broken
gnarled arch carried in times of old, and because
the living give no offerings,
instead there shall live, from within it,
this supple, new-born beast.

Already there is no one who waits, or protects.
No sound emerges from the flute.
The chattering wind blew it away.
Down below, the enormous stomach
quakes with human torment,
once again lifting its ridge:
the vipers, hissing to the new
century's golden tempo.

[OM]

NEAR

Should I look at the winter trees before the window,
the frost-beaten twilight, instead of your body?
Should I slowly sip my scalding hot drink?
Twilight, the clink of cups, clattering
of the dictation machine. I'm not interested
if there is any meaning to suffering,
what is created by regret,
or what shall remain of art
if no rules are valid
any more. I fear only blindness.
Very often I awaken at dawn.
There is no fear in me, but still
a feeling whispers: the time is drawing near

when we will have to find words
for what lies beyond the boundary,
and we will have to give account
of what ruptured in us, while embracing.

LIGHT OF NIGHT-TIME

As long as that suffocating desire to bind yourself
in one body exists, there can be only self-betrayal,
self-attack in that distance which never will fit
your steps: you cannot traverse it. Suddenly, in the
middle of the night, a desire to flee. Outside, the wind
sweeps all along the lost monochrome world,
turning over garbage bins in front of the houses. Countless scraps
of paper spills out of them, plastic bottles,
moldy breadcrusts, the remnants of lives
destitute and squandering. Now you can choose a direction. Your step
is brisker than in daytime. You wonder why
there is so much traffic at night. Beneath the bridge's new lighting,
cars glide along, trams run by. But below,

it's as if the river has stopped. You look down, the depths
pierce you as if hit by a bullet. Darkness would enter you,
fully. You are grateful to the bridge, which, from concrete and iron,
pries open an illusion. But you can't ask for an eye
on loan, which, releasing the shutter for hours,
looks at a face, the dark masses of the houses on both sides
of the river — and there is no one to whom you could give
this emptiness. The lights of the evening bear
the seal of history like too delicate skin,
every wound remaining, and in vain does imagination
rise again, the body moves slowly, too late —
only when the world is lost to it.

[OM]

RETURN OF THE LETTERS

One evening, the vagrant letters returned to the house
behind the dam. The water had sealed it off
from the village: debris, dead leaves, pigeon-carcasses
rotted away inside, generations of cats proliferating
between the piss-soaked rafters.

The letters still remembered the hands
which had set them in place, and they wandered
across every page, like the cats roaming over every ruinous
nook and cranny, from one margin to the other. First the letter

s

came in through an opening in the window. Sensing
the feline reek, in a terrible voice it began to yell,

may the wind blow upon you, wafts of air
and tornados: as it screamed, the plank
on which it stood wobbled. Hearing the clamor
two elderly tomcats jumped out. They arched
their backs, and the first letter retreated, tripping
on a shard of tile, falling down. In the meantime,
imperceptibly, the second letter crept in,

P.

It stared and stared at the pigeon cadavers. They
had become like greasy piles of rags, and as
it looked, it thought back upon a bespectacled countenance,
eyes exactly the same color of grey, and the hand as well,
as it went along the page from row to row,
the same shade of grey. It then stepped
over the debris and rotting mud to the door,

nearly pushing it from its hinges, and
the evening sun etched itself into the house. The letter

D

was the last to arrive. It played in the doorway with a spotted kitten,
rolled it onto its belly, played hide-and-seek
around its legs, then settled down on a broken-edged
stone bench, for a long time could not fall
asleep. It was a warm summer evening. Above the dam,
the Moon appeared like a grey eye.

LOVE, SAIL, TIME

Everything that can — ascends to the sky.
The chimney's smoke, a prayer,
happiness, and mourning.
Everything that can swims away into the distance.
Childhood, love, sail, time.
And still they stand here.
They stand here, and they know that they will pay.
With happiness, with mourning, with love.
They stand here, protecting hope, and time,
everything frail like a flower stalk,
like a meeting beneath the torn summer clouds,
like a kiss on the eyes of the sick.
And already, here is the one who does not tolerate this anarchy.

The one who wants order,
the one who brings money, promises, weapons.
Who has arrived here, offended.
He is here and threatening.
And everything that can ascends to the sky.
But still they stand here,
they do not move.
And with them there remains: childhood,
love, sail, and time.

RENDING

1

A telephone call? Or was it a message? I don't recall. At the funeral the rain was cascading down, and the speeches enraged me so much that I would have been happy to hit someone.

Accept me today as one
Who shall partake of Thy mystical supper.

Everyone wanted to know what happened. When and how you did it. Someone said the whole thing was like a Greek tragedy. Someone else said you'd planned it all down to the tiniest detail.

Accept me today as one
Who shall partake of Thy mystical supper.

From the funeral chapel, wind-battered umbrellas proceeded toward the grave. In front was the priest, who, behold, made an exception for you.

Accept me today as one
Who shall partake of Thy mystical supper.

I stared at the pebbles in front of my feet. I kept shoving them around with the tip of my shoe. I dared not look at those you had left behind here, left behind here as your own dead, so that we would always ask: how we had wronged you, what we had done against you.

Accept me today as one
Who shall partake of Thy mystical supper.

Finally, the house where you hanged yourself. Small pastries and stuffed cabbage awaited the company. Food was offered & taken. But I looked for the place where you tied the noose — where was that place, where was the hook — I had to see it so as not to be party to that deed.

2

Then the trip back. To the city, from where you had fled. Darkness clattering beneath my eyelids. Eight years of silence began.

How do we bid farewell to the one
we can never speak to again —

I still did not know that in my lungs, between the ribs, pepper-sized tumors were growing. I was raising death half from things, half from fears, another death to place next to your own; just as, long ago, I gathered bird names for you as I walked in a German forest: blaumeise, buchfink, buntspecht, zaunkönig, waldbaumläufer, zilpzalp.

How do we bid farewell to the one
we can never speak to again —

At the time I lived in a narrow dark room, going out only when I had nothing left to eat. The window looked onto the back wall of a bank building with a metal staircase. The entire day, some kind of terrible machine made a buzzing sound. Like some grinder with its enormous maw. I don't know what it was, I don't know what was happening in the interior of this machine, just as I don't know what those suicidal cells conveyed, within you, to the soul about to depart when the air pipe closed, the vertebra cracked from the convulsions, but still there were ten or fifteen minutes when those last cells, still living, exploded one after the other, panicking: the death of the heart set in, and at last there remained only the soulless flesh.

How do we bid farewell to the one
we can never speak to again —

In those ten or fifteen minutes every voice grew silent; every letter, the open and the closed, gave themselves back to the fear which filled the world before the very first letter, Bet, which means house, was born from the light, and opened the path for the others. Now it gave itself back to the dark, and the house remained empty; its body no longer gave any sounds.

How do we bid farewell to the one
we can never speak to again —

That is when the silence began in me. Because how should the one remaining here speak? Every morning, a crow descended to a tree across from my bed; I watched as it preened on the branches of the morning tree, I delighted in it, I delighted in those whom I love. This is how I remained here in this wasteland, like the Chukchis in their own hopeless land. Whoever remains here is not the sign of anything. Only a sign left by the dead — and in every sign there is another death.

3

I lay on the table, waiting for the operation, my chest shaved bare, I was trembling from the cold, and I'd never felt so tranquil as then, when at last I could give my life into the hands of others, and I could do nothing for myself.

My Lord, as you were raised to the cross,
fear and trembling seized every creature.

If anyone asked about you, I answered nothing. But I spoke to you many times within myself. At first I felt fear, the fear of the last hours, fear of what you went through. I called forth that image in my head as, palms facing downward, you place your hands beneath your thighs, you tilt back & forth on the chair, you mutter something to yourself, I try to understand what you are trying to say but I can't — then in the end we embrace each other.

My Lord, as you were raised to the cross,
fear and trembling seized every creature.

Then anger took the place of fear. It was easier that way. How many times and in how many ways you misled me, how you kept building the despairing theatre of your suffering, how you sent out simultaneously true and false signs of reality which made me feel that I am not rushing towards you when I should be rushing towards you, I am not keeping vigil when you are calling upon me to keep vigil, and when, at long last, I reached you — you just smiled and said that there were, there are no problems.

My Lord, as you were raised to the cross,
fear and trembling seized every creature.

During these eight years, the time has never come when the pain would withdraw back into the signs, or release within the signs he who signifies pain. What would be needed for the pain to fall asleep within the signs, like the bulbs in the earth, like the cypress trees, the ivy's poisonous green beneath the beneficent snow? What would be needed so that, from that emptiness into which you threw yourself, there would begin to trickle, as from a dried well — grace.

My Lord, as you were raised to the cross,
fear and trembling seized every creature.

And what remains to the one here, the carrier of signs, but who can never become a sign for himself? The demon of empty depths attacks him like a ravenous mosquito at night. It buzzes around his head like lunacy. How ridiculous is the resident of the body who casts his word-net into the emptiness; how empty his silence. It is not the word, the voice, and not silence that redeems the body from the body, the soul from the soul.

4

It is Easter, Holy Thursday. I read news of the war: in the mass graves, doctors performing autopsies have found pointed steel projectiles three and four centimeters long; they become hook-shaped after sinking into the body. One missile can release eight thousand of these projectiles, covering the entire target area.

Encompassed by the uttermost depths of sin,
no longer able to endure its stormy waves,
as Jonah from the whale I cry out to Thee:
Lead me up from ruin.

And as I write this, from the leaden black sky, the rain is cascading down. Just as it was then.

Encompassed by the uttermost depths of sin,
no longer able to endure its stormy waves,
as Jonah from the whale I cry out to Thee:
Lead me up from ruin.

I wanted to live. Even when I could no longer get any
air, and I whispered: I am ruined. I wanted to live a
little longer yet in this parched, half-finished after-
world — I remained here, nailed up onto lack, within
the half-things, within the fears, prepared to embrace,
like the boy who did not claim his father's inheritance,
he never went anywhere, he ran after the flock, he
patched the roof, he struggled with wild animals, all
these tasks which, if he had not existed, any servant
could have completed just as well in his place.

Encompassed by the uttermost depths of sin,
no longer able to endure its stormy waves,
as Jonah from the whale I cry out to Thee:
Lead me up from ruin.

So now here I am. There is war: women are raped, infants are murdered.

Encompassed by the uttermost depths of sin,
no longer able to endure its stormy waves,
as Jonah from the whale I cry out to Thee:
Lead me up from ruin.

You don't see this, you don't hear this anymore. Help me, if you can; help me to remain a servant, not a deceiver, until I am inscribed into the final sign — the community of bodies, the humiliated earth.

[OM]

PREVIOUS PUBLICATIONS

"Canvases of Time," "Margin," "From beneath the Letters," and "Sinking Island" translated by Ottilie Mulzet, were published in *Metamorphoses* (Spring/Summer 2022).

"To My Dead" and "Third Day Unceasingly," translated by Ottilie Mulzet, were published in *Two Lines* (2022).

"Dust," translated by Ottilie Mulzet, was read by the author at the Literature Live Around the World 2022 Bergen Literary Festival.

"Diagrams in the River" is an epigraph to Gábor Schein's *Autobiographies of an Angel*, translated by Ottilie Mulzet (Yale University Press, Margellos World Republic of Letters, June 2022).

"Preparations for a City," "Beyond the Cordons," "Come Back," translated by Ottilie Mulzet; and "Invisible War," translated by Erika Mihálycsa, were published on lyrikline.de (2020).

"Captain Cornelius's Letter from Pannonia to Burrus in the Colonial Office in Rome" and "The Taste of Salt," translated by Erika Mihálycsa, were published in *Asymptote Journal* (2018).

"Invisible War," translated by Erika Mihálycsa, was published in *World Literature Today* (Jan. 2017).

"Farewell, Russian Style," "Beyond the Cordons," "Note on the Back of a Map," "Atropos's Scissors," "Dawn Light," and "Above the Gravel Path," translated by Ottilie Mulzet, were published in almostisland.com (Spring 2015).

"With Eyes Turned Inside Out" translated by Erika Mihálycsa, was published by *Trafika Europe 5* (2015).

"After the Iron Age," translated by Erika Mihálycsa, was published in *The Missing Slate* (2015).

"Preparation for the Crows' Feast," translated by Ottilie Mulzet, was published in *The Missing Slate* (2015).

"Come Back" and "Gravel and Reeds," translated by Ottilie Mulzet, were published in *Two Lines 23* (Fall 2015).

"Ghost Homeland," originally entitled "The Day after Christmas," translated by Ottilie Mulzet, was published on *Hungarian Literature Online* (hlo.hu) in 2012.

"The Builders of the Garden," translated by Ottilie Mulzet, was originally published on *Hungarian Literature Online* (hlo.hu) in 2009.

"Return of the Letters" and "Margin," translated by Ottilie Mulzet, were originally published on *Hungarian Literature Online* (hlo.hu) in 2009.

BIOGRAPHIES

Gábor Schein is the highly acclaimed author of over nine volumes of poetry and five novels. He has been awarded the Attila József Prize, the Artisjus Prize, and the Prize of the Society of Hungarian Authors, among many other distinctions. His work has been translated into eight European languages. His other works in English include the short novels *The Book of Mordechai* (tr. Adam Z. Levy) and *Lazarus* (tr. Ottilie Mulzet; Seagull Books, 2017), and his novel *Autobiographies of an Angel* (tr. Ottilie Mulzet, Yale University Press, 2022).

Ottilie Mulzet has translated over fifteen volumes of Hungarian poetry & prose, including works by Szilárd Borbély, László Krasznahorkai, Gábor Schein, György Dragomán, László Földényi, Krisztina Tóth, Edina Szvoren, and others. Her translation of Krasznahorkai's *Baron Wenckheim's Homecoming* was awarded the 2019 National Book Award in Translated Literature. An anthology of modern poetry by Hungarian women (with other translators), *Under a Pannonian Sky: Ten Women Poets from Hungary*, is forthcoming from Seagull Books in 2025.

Erika Mihálycsa teaches modern and contemporary English literature at Babes-Bolyai University, Cluj, Romania. She is the author of the monograph *'A wretchedness to defend': Reading Beckett's Letters* (2022), co-editor of *Retranslating Joyce for the 21st Century* (2020), and editor of Rareș Moldovan's new, annotated Romanian translation of Joyce's *Ulysses* (2023). She has translated fiction by Beckett, Flann O'Brien, Patrick McCabe and others into Hungarian as well as translating Hungarian authors into English, most importantly, two novels by the experimental modernist Miklós Szentkuthy, published by Contra Mundum Press.

COLOPHON

BEYOND THE CORDONS
was handset in InDesign CC.

The text font is *BC Figural*.

The display font is *Antikva Margaret*.

Book design & typesetting: Alessandro Segalini

Cover design: CMP

Front cover image: Brassaï, *Graffiti* (1950).
Silver gelatin print, 9.4" × 6.9".

Opening image: Emila Medková, *Explosion* (1959).
Black & white photograph. Artist's estate © Eva Kosáková

BEYOND THE CORDONS
is published by Contra Mundum Press.

Contra Mundum Press New York · London · Melbourne

CONTRA MUNDUM PRESS

Dedicated to the value & the indispensable importance of the individual voice, to works that test the boundaries of thought & experience.

The primary aim of Contra Mundum is to publish translations of writers who in their use of form and style are *à rebours*, or who deviate significantly from more programmatic & spurious forms of experimentation. Such writing attests to the volatile nature of modernism. Our preference is for works that have not yet been translated into English, are out of print, or are poorly translated, for writers whose thinking & æsthetics are in opposition to timely or mainstream currents of thought, value systems, or moralities. We also reprint obscure and out-of-print works we consider significant but which have been forgotten, neglected, or overshadowed.

There are many works of fundamental significance to *Weltliteratur* (& *Weltkultur*) that still remain in relative oblivion, works that alter and disrupt standard circuits of thought — these warrant being encountered by the world at large. It is our aim to render them more visible.

For the complete list of forthcoming publications, please visit our website. To be added to our mailing list, send your name and email address to: info@contramundum.net

Contra Mundum Press
P.O. Box 1326
New York, NY 10276
USA

OTHER CONTRA MUNDUM PRESS TITLES

2012 *Gilgamesh*
Ghérasim Luca, *Self-Shadowing Prey*
Rainer J. Hanshe, *The Abdication*
Walter Jackson Bate, *Negative Capability*
Miklós Szentkuthy, *Marginalia on Casanova*
Fernando Pessoa, *Philosophical Essays*
2013 Elio Petri, *Writings on Cinema & Life*
Friedrich Nietzsche, *The Greek Music Drama*
Richard Foreman, *Plays with Films*
Louis-Auguste Blanqui, *Eternity by the Stars*
Miklós Szentkuthy, *Towards the One & Only Metaphor*
Josef Winkler, *When the Time Comes*
2014 William Wordsworth, *Fragments*
Josef Winkler, *Natura Morta*
Fernando Pessoa, *The Transformation Book*
Emilio Villa, *The Selected Poetry of Emilio Villa*
Robert Kelly, *A Voice Full of Cities*
Pier Paolo Pasolini, *The Divine Mimesis*
Miklós Szentkuthy, *Prae, Vol. 1*
2015 Federico Fellini, *Making a Film*
Robert Musil, *Thought Flights*
Sándor Tar, *Our Street*
Lorand Gaspar, *Earth Absolute*
Josef Winkler, *The Graveyard of Bitter Oranges*
Ferit Edgü, *Noone*
Jean-Jacques Rousseau, *Narcissus*
Ahmad Shamlu, *Born Upon the Dark Spear*
2016 Jean-Luc Godard, *Phrases*
Otto Dix, *Letters, Vol. 1*
Maura Del Serra, *Ladder of Oaths*
Pierre Senges, *The Major Refutation*
Charles Baudelaire, *My Heart Laid Bare & Other Texts*
2017 Joseph Kessel, *Army of Shadows*
Rainer J. Hanshe & Federico Gori, *Shattering the Muses*
Gérard Depardieu, *Innocent*
Claude Mouchard, *Entangled — Papers! — Notes*

2018	Miklós Szentkuthy, *Black Renaissance*
	Adonis & Pierre Joris, *Conversations in the Pyrenees*
2019	Charles Baudelaire, *Belgium Stripped Bare*
	Robert Musil, *Unions*
	Iceberg Slim, *Night Train to Sugar Hill*
	Marquis de Sade, *Aline & Valcour*
2020	*A City Full of Voices: Essays on the Work of Robert Kelly*
	Rédoine Faïd, *Outlaw*
	Carmelo Bene, *I Appeared to the Madonna*
	Paul Celan, *Microliths They Are, Little Stones*
	Zsuzsa Selyem, *It's Raining in Moscow*
	Bérengère Viennot, *Trumpspeak*
	Robert Musil, *Theater Symptoms*
	Miklós Szentkuthy, *Chapter on Love*
2021	Charles Baudelaire, *Paris Spleen*
	Marguerite Duras, *The Darkroom*
	Andrew Dickos, *Honor Among Thieves*
	Pierre Senges, *Ahab (Sequels)*
	Carmelo Bene, *Our Lady of the Turks*
2022	Fernando Pessoa, *Writings on Art & Poetical Theory*
	Miklós Szentkuthy, *Prae, Vol. 2*
	Blixa Bargeld, *Europe Crosswise: A Litany*
	Pierre Joris, *Always the Many, Never the One*
	Robert Musil, *Literature & Politics*
2023	Pierre Joris, *Interglacial Narrows*
	Gabriele Tinti, *Bleedings — Incipit Tragœdia*
	Évelyne Grossman, *The Creativity of the Crisis*
	Rainer J. Hanshe, *Closing Melodies*
	Kari Hukkila, *One Thousand & One*
2024	Antonin Artaud, *Journey to Mexico*
	Rainer J. Hanshe, *Dionysos Speed*
	Amina Saïd, *Walking the Earth*

SOME FORTHCOMING TITLES

Nuriá Perpinyà, *And, Suddenly, Paradise*
Marquis de Sade, *Stories, Tales, & Fables*

AGRODOLCE SERIES Æ

2020 Dejan Lukić, *The Oyster*
2022 Ugo Tognazzi, *The Injester*

2006–PRESENT

To read samples and order current & back issues of *Hyperion*,
visit contramundumpress.com/hyperion
Edited by Rainer J. Hanshe & Erika Mihálycsa (2014 ~)

is published by Rainer J. Hanshe
Typography & Design: Alessandro Segalini
Publicity & Marketing: Alexandra Gold
Fundraising & Grant Writing: Madeline Hausmann
Ebook Design: Carlie R. Houser

THE FUTURE OF KULCHUR

THE PROJECT

From major museums like the MoMA to art house cinemas such as Film Forum, cultural organizations do not sustain themselves from sales alone, but from subscriptions, donations, benefactors, and grants.

Since benefactors of Peggy Guggenheim's stature are rare to come by, and receiving large grants from major funding bodies is an infrequent and unreliable source of capital, we seek to further our venture through a form of modest support that is within everyone's reach.

Although esteemed, Contra Mundum is an independent boutique press with modest profit margins. In not having university, state, or institutional backing, other forms of sustenance are required to move us into the future.

Additionally, in the past decade, the reduction of the purchasing budgets across the nation of both public and private libraries has had a severe impact upon publishers, leading to significant decreases in sales, thereby necessitating the creation of alternative means of subsistence.

Because many of our books are translations, our desire for proper remuneration is a persistent point of concern. Even when translators receive grants for book projects, the amount is often insufficient to compensate for their efforts, and royalties, which trickle in slowly over years, are not a reliable source of compensation.

WHAT WILL BE DONE

With your participation we seek to offer writers and translators greater compensation for their work, and in a more expeditious manner.

Additionally, funds will be used to pay for translation rights, basic operating expenses of the press, and to represent our writers and translators at book fairs.

If the means exist, we will also create a translation residency, providing opportunities to both junior and more established translators, thereby furthering our cultural efforts.

Through a greater collective and the cultural commons of the world, we can band together to create this constellation and together function as a patron for the writers and artists published by CMP. We hope you will join us in this partnership.

Your patronage is an expression of your confidence and belief in visionary literary work that would otherwise be exiled from the Anglophone world. With bookstores and presses around the world struggling to survive, and many even closing, joining the Future of Kulchur allows you to be a part of an active force that forms a continuous *&* stable foundation which safeguards the longevity of Contra Mundum Press.

Endowed by your support, we can expand our poetics of hospitality by continuing to publish works from many different languages and reflect, welcome, and embrace the riches of other cultures throughout the world. To become a member of any of our Future of Kulchur tiers is to express your support of such cultural work, and to aid us in continuing it. A unified assemblage of individuals can make a modern Mæcenas and deepen access to radical works.

The Oyster ($2/month)

- Three issues (PDFs) of your choice of our art journal, *Hyperion*.
- 15% discount on all purchases (for orders made directly through our site) during the subscription term (one year).
- Impact: $2 a month contributes to the cost to convert a title to an ebook and make it accessible to wider audiences.

Paris Spleen ($5/month)

- Receive $35 worth of books or your choice from our back catalog.
- Three issues (PDFs) of your choice of our art journal, *Hyperion*.
- 18% discount on all purchases (for orders made directly through our site) during the subscription term (one year).
- Impact: $5 a month contributes to the cost purchasing new fonts for expanding the range of our typesetting palette.

Gilgamesh ($10/month)

- Receive $70 worth books of your choice from our back catalog.
- 4 PDF issues of our magazine *Hyperion*.
- A quarterly newsletter with exclusive content such as interviews with authors or translators, excerpts from upcoming titles, publication news, and more.
- 20% discount on all merchandise (for orders made directly through our site) during the subscription term (one year).
- Select images of our books as they are being typeset.
- Impact: $10 a month contributes to the production and publication of *Hyperion*, encouraging critical engagement with art theory & æsthetics and ensuring we can pay our contributors.

The Greek Music Drama ($25/month)

- Receive $215 worth of books.
- 5 PDF issues of *Hyperion* ($25 value).
- A quarterly newsletter with exclusive content such as interviews with authors or translators, excerpts from upcoming titles, publication news, and more.
- 25% discount (for orders made directly through our site) on all merchandise during the subscription term (one year).
- Impact: $25 a month contributes to the cost of designing and formatting a book.

Citizen Above Suspicion ($50/month)

- Receive $525 worth of books.
- 6 PDF issues of *Hyperion* ($30 value).
- 1 tote.
- A quarterly newsletter with exclusive content such as interviews with authors or translators, excerpts from upcoming titles, publication news, and more.
- 30% discount on all merchandise (for orders made directly through our site) during the subscription term (one year).
- Select one forthcoming book from our catalog and receive it in advance of release to the general public.
- Impact: $50 a month contributes to editorial & proofreading fees.

Casanova ($100/month)

- Receive $1040 worth of books.
- 7 PDF issues of *Hyperion* ($30 value).
- 1 tote.
- A quarterly newsletter with exclusive content such as interviews with authors or translators, excerpts from upcoming titles, publication news, and more.
- 35% discount on all merchandise (for orders made directly through our site) during the subscription term (one year).
- A signed typeset spread from two forthcoming books.
- Select two forthcoming books from our catalog and receive them in advance of release to the general public.
- Impact: $100 a month contributes to the cost of translating a book, therefore supporting a translator in their craft & bringing a new work & perspective to Anglophone audiences.

Cybernetogamic Vampire ($200/month)

- Receive $2020 worth of books.
- 10 PDF issues of *Hyperion* ($50 value).
- 1 tote.
- A quarterly newsletter with exclusive content such as interviews with authors or translators, excerpts from upcoming titles, publication news, and more.
- 40% discount on all merchandise (for orders made directly through our site) during the subscription term (one year).
- A signed typeset spread from four of our forthcoming books.
- The listing of your name in the colophon to a forthcoming book of your choice.
- Select four forthcoming books from our catalog and receive them in advance of release to the general public.
- Impact: $200 a month contributes to general operating expenses of the press, paying for translation rights, and attending book fairs to represent our writers and translators and reach more readers around the world.

To join the Future of Kulchur, visit here:

contramundumpress.com/support-us

www.ingramcontent.com/pod-product-compliance
Lightning Source LLC
Chambersburg PA
CBHW020850160426
43192CB00007B/867